The Complete Beginners Guide
X Sierra (Version 10.12)

(For MacBook, MacBook Air, MacBook Pro, iMac, Mac Pro, and Mac Mini)

By Scott La Counte

Table of Contents

Introduction

Every year or so you hear the big pitch: Windows is *finally* going to be awesome again. The new update is big, grander and a huge overhaul. And then it comes and it's more buggy, weirder, and less functional than the version that came before! That's probably what made you consider making the switch—you're tired of the excuses and you want a computer that just works!

Whether you are a new convert to Mac, still thinking about making the switch, or just want to learn more about Macs, this book will guide you through the Mac OS and help you see how making the switch really isn't the great leap that you once thought it was.

This book will show you the basics and show you how to do the common day tasks you know on Windows (like right clicking). It will also show you how to get your Mac in sync with your iPad or iPhone, and how to do everyday tasks like change background, find files, and performance tweaks to keep your Mac running like new.

This book is based off of OS Sierra (released September 20, 2016)

What's New In Sierra?

If you are upgrading from OS Yosemite or OS El Capitan, you'll quickly notice one thing: it looks almost exactly the same. That's because most of the changes were under the hood; the OS is built to run quicker, but the look and feel is largely unchanged.

That's not to say nothing is changed. There are hundreds of minor changes and updates. The biggest enhancement is Siri integration; facial recognition to photos; Apple Pay; new effects to Messages; picture in picture video play; and a universal clipboard that lets you copy something from your Mac onto your iPhone.

If you bought a new Macbook or Macbook Pro (Macbook Air is not yet compatible), then there's a good chance a Force Touch track pad was included; Force Touch lets you do different gestures based on how firm you touch the mouse. It will covered in great depth later in the book.

Mac? Is It Worth It?

Before diving into the actual software, let's address the obvious: why pick Mac?

I was in the Windows camp for a long time; I'd see the Mac and think it was just a computer for hipsters. Sure they were nice to look at—they were shiny and didn't look plastic-y and cheap…but they were also expensive.

But then I actually used one, and I was blown away. Here's why…

Fewer Viruses
You've probably heard someone say they use a Mac because they don't get viruses. That's not true. Any computer can get a virus. But it is true that Macs are generally less prone to viruses and are more secure.

The reason you don't hear about Mac viruses very often is twofold:
1. While it's hard to pinpoint just how many computers there are in the world, most estimates say less than 10% of the world's computers are Macs. Most computers are still Windows. So if you are a hacker wanting to wreak havoc into cyberspace, then your obvious target would be the one with the largest audience.
2. The second reason is Mac OS is built by Apple, for Apple. Windows builds their OS to be built for essentially any computer, which opens the door for vulnerabilities.

I know a lot of Mac users, and rarely do I hear someone say they have a virus. If you are concerned, however, one popular free virus protector is called Bitdefender Virus Scanner (http://www.bitdefender.com/).

Keeping It Simple
When it comes to design, Apple likes to make things that are beautiful and simple. This philosophy can be seen in their watches, iPhones, and iPads—across all their products.

Because Apple spends so much time keeping it simple, you also have seen the last days of computer crashes and blue screens of deaths.

Apple spends a lot of time thinking not just about what the computer should do, but how people will do it. If you've been using Windows all of your life, then all the different menus and buttons might seem intimidating at first—but don't stress! This book will show you how much easier it actually is.

If you have any other Apple product, then many of the common Mac tasks will probably seem very similar to you. What's more, if you have an iPhone, iPad, or even Apple TV, then they all work and interact with each other.

No Bloat
I remember my last Windows computer. I couldn't wait to turn it on…and then I couldn't wait to turn it off! Your first hour should be spent just having fun exploring it, but my first hour was spent uninstalling programs!

One reason Windows computers are cheaper is because manufacturers team up with software companies and install all kinds of unnecessary programs—most of them are just free trials.

With Mac, you turn your computer on for the first time, create an ID if you don't already have one, put in your Wi-Fi, and login to iTunes / iCloud. That's it. It should take less than ten minutes to get your computer up and running once you get it out of the box.

Installation

First things first: installation. If you have a new computer, then this won't apply to you; your computer is already setup with the most recent OS (operating system). Because Apple constantly updates their software, however, you will want to see if there's an update available.

To do that, just go to your Launchpad (It's the rocket in the taskbar at the bottom of your screen), and click it once.

This brings up all your currently installed apps. You can either type "App" to search for the App Store, or you can just look for the icon. If there's an update available, you'll see a number on it, which represents how many updates are available.

To see the update, click the icon (and notice I don't say right click or left click? That's because there's only one kind of click on Mac, unlike Windows).

Next, click "Updates" from the top menu bar, and then click "Update" next to the software that needs updating. If you don't see an Update button, then you are all set—no update is needed. If you do update, depending on the size of the update and speed of your Internet, it will usually take ten to forty minutes to update—and it will need to restart your computer to fully install. While it's updating, you can continue using your computer—it will tell you before it restarts so you can save your work. The OS will do everything for you—the only thing you need to do during the update is wait for it to complete.

Apple will generally release a new OS each year (traditionally around the same time that new iPhones are announced), but there will be several updates throughout the year; you might see one or two that adds new features, but most of them are security updates or under the hood.

OS X 10.9 Mavericks

If you are using an older computer and need to install the latest OS (Sierra), it's pretty simple. Just go to the app store just mentioned, and search for Sierra, then download it. Here's the good news about the update: it's free! Apple has done away with charging for software updates.

The file is just over 5 GB in size so make sure your computer has room—if it doesn't you can skip ahead a few sections and see how to clean up your Mac. Once it's finished downloading, follow the on-screen prompts. Your Mac will restart several times, so don't worry about it acting weird—this is normal.

You'll know when it's finished because everything will look a lot different, you'll have cool new wallpaper, and a Welcome dialogue box will appear.

OS X 10.8 Mountain Lion or Below

If you are one of the few Mac users who haven't yet upgraded to OS X Mavericks and are still using OS X Snow Leopard, Lion, or Mountain Lion, you will have to finally bite the bullet and click the download link for Sierra.

Here's the bad news for you: if your computer has an OS that is less than Mavericks, there's a very good chance it doesn't support Sierra.

The general requirements are below:

- At least 2 GB RAM or more
- At least 9 GB of available hard drive storage
- iMac 2009 or later
- MacBook 2009 and later
- MacBook Pro 2010 or later
- MacBook Air 2010 or later
- Mac Mini 2010 or later
- Mac Pro 2010 or later

You can see your computer specs by going to the very upper left corner of your screen and clicking on the little apple, and then clicking on "About This Mac".

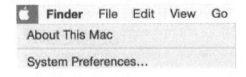

This will tell you all the information that you want to know (i.e. the year your Mac came out, the speed, the memory, etc.).

Mac vs. Windows

So exactly how is Mac different from Windows? Throughout the book I'll be making comparisons to help you, but first I want to give a rundown of some of the major differences.

Right Click
Right clicking is probably second nature to you if you are a Windows user; on the Mac, it's all about gestures—touching the trackpad (the Mac's mouse) a certain way (or on new Macs, using more or less pressure) will bring up different options and menus.

As weird as it sounds, the first time I used a Mac, the right click (or lack thereof) drove me crazy…until I figured out that right clicking was actually there. To right click on a Mac, click with two fingers instead of one. Alternatively, you can press Control and with one finger.

If you have an old Windows USB mouse, you don't have to toss it—you can plug it into your Mac and it will work with no installation. The right click will even work.

I'll explain how to customize your TrackPad later in the book, but if you'd like to jump ahead, you can go to System Preferences>TrackPad.

And don't worry about messing something up; it's very hard to harm a Mac!

Keyboard Shortcuts
This section will give you a very quick rundown of the more popular keyboard shortcuts; for a more detailed list, see Appendix A at the end of this book.

On a Windows computer, you might be used to using Control (CTRL) frequently; Control is on the Mac keyboard, but don't get confused—on a Mac, the Control button equivalent is the Command (⌘) Key (to the right of the keyboard). The good news is the letter combination for the most frequently used Windows shortcuts is almost always the same on a Mac—Control-C to copy is Command-C on the Mac; Control-X to Cut is Command-X; Control-V to Paste is Command-V.

On a Windows computer, you can hold Alt and Tab to cycle through programs…on a Mac you use Command and Tab.

The two most frequently used function keys (the buttons above the numbers) are F3 and F4; F3 will show a list of the programs you have open, and F4 brings up your Launchpad (all of your available programs…kind of like the Start menu on Windows).

Just keep reminding yourself that while it looks different, it's really not…Windows has File Explorer, Mac has Finder; Windows has the Start Menu, Mac has Launchpad; Windows has the Ribbon menu, Mac has the Top Navigation menu.

Below is a quick overview of what things are called on Windows and what they are called on a Mac:

Windows	Mac
Windows Explorer / My Computer / Computer	Finder
Control Panel	System Preferences
Programs	Applications (often shortened to apps)
Task Bar and Start Menu	Dock
Tray	Menulets
Recycle Bin	Trash
Task Manager	Activity Monitor
Windows Phone's Action Center (Windows 10 Feature)	Notification Center
Media Center	iTunes

Transferring Documents

The thing a lot of people worry about when updating any computer is how to get all of your information from your old computer to your new computer. With Macs, it's a pretty simple task—you can even take it into your local Apple Store for free help (appointments are needed, so don't just walk in).

If you don't want to wait for an appointment or you just like doing things on your own, there's already a tool on your computer to help: it's called Migration Assistant. Be advised you do need an Internet connection.

To start, go to your Windows computer and either search any search engine for "Windows Migration Assistant" or go directly to https://support.apple.com/kb/DL1557?locale=en_US. Once you are there, download and install the program on your Windows computer.

Windows Migration Assistant v1.0.5.7
Download

This software will help you migrate data from a Windows PC running Windows XP, Windows Vista, Windows 7 or Windows 8. The Migration Assistant will launch automatically after it has been installed.

For more information, please see http://support.apple.com/kb/HT4796.

From your Mac, click the Launchpad icon (i.e. the rocket on your taskbar).

Next click on Other and then click Migration Assistant.

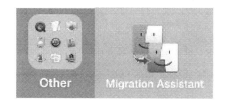

To use Migration Assistant, everything that is open on your Mac will be closed, so make sure and save your work, and don't start until you are ready.

From the setup, click Continue, and then select "From another Mac, PC, Time Machine backup, or other disk," then select Continue and then "From another Mac or PC." The next window should show the Windows computer that you want to transfer files from. Click Continue, verify on the Windows computer that the passcodes match and click Continue again. Lastly, the assistant will ask you to select the types of files you want to transfer.

If you don't do the assistant right away, you can always use it later. There's no timeline for using it, so if you dig up an older Windows computer in the garage and want to transfer everything from it, the option will always be there.

Compatibility

Now that you have everything copied over, let's talk briefly about compatibility. While many files will open on a Mac, software will *not*. That means if you have Word on your Windows, you can't just move it over; most popular software (like Word) is available on the Mac, but you will have to purchase it.

Don't stress too much; most the files that you have just transferred will actually still open even if you don't buy software to open them. Word files (Doc, Docx) for example, will open in Pages (which is free on new Macs, and is $19.99 on older ones).

If your file does not open, then you will probably be able to find free software online that will open it.

Setup Assistant

If you are starting up the Mac for the first time (and you are the first owner), then the first thing that will happen is an automated setup assistant will guide you through creating an account and getting everything set up.

The first thing you'll do is select your country; if you don't see yours, then click "See All." Click "Continue" after you finish each section. Next you'll choose your keyboard layout; if you are an English speaker, then United States is probably your first bet, but if you are going to be typing primarily in another language (like Chinese) then you may want to pick that country instead—this can be changed later.

Picking the wireless network is the next thing you will see after clicking Continue—you don't have to set up wireless at this point, but if you do it will also trigger the Migration Assistant (which will help you transfer files); this is all optional so you can skip it (you can also come back to it later).

The next screen is one of the most important: entering your Apple ID. If you have any other Apple device (iPad, iPod, iPhone, etc.) or if you have an ID that you use with Windows, then you'll want to use it because all of the apps, music and other media you've paid for are tied to your account. If you don't have one, you'll have the option of getting one—it's free and includes iCloud (also free), which will be talked about more later.

The next part of the setup is Find My Mac (which you need iCloud for); this is a great feature that lets you see where your Mac is from your Internet browser; if it's been stolen it also lets you wipe away all of your content.

After agreeing to the terms, you'll be taken to the Time Zone selection. After that you are asked if you want to enable the iCloud Keychain. What's the iCloud Keychain? Basically, this stores passwords in the cloud so you can use them on any device.

Next, decide if you want to send diagnostics and usage data to Apple; this all for statistical purposes to help Apple make their software and hardware better, but it's entirely up to you. It won't slow your computer down if you do decide to do it—it's all done in the background. After this step you decide if you want to register your installation with Apple.

Finally, you are ready to start using your Mac!

Part I: Mac OS Crash Course

Keyboard

The keyboard?! I know what you're thinking: a keyboard is a keyboard! Well, sort of. While it is true that you could use a Windows keyboard on a Mac, there are keyboards (including the one that's free with your Mac or built into your MacBook) that are specifically designed for Mac.

There are not a lot of differences; below are the four main ones.

Apple Key
On a Windows keyboard, there is a button that looks like a Windows flag called the Windows Button. There's no sense putting a Windows button on a Mac keyboard, so where the Windows button normally is, you'll find the Apple button, which doesn't look at all like an apple! It actually looks like this (⌘); it's more commonly known as the Command Button—though some people also call it the Clover Key and Pretzel Key.

Delete (Backspace)
On a Windows keyboard, the backspace button is a 'Backwards Delete' key and the delete button is a 'Forward Delete' key (removing the space immediately after the cursor). On a Mac keyboard, the backspace key is labeled 'Delete' and is in exactly the same location as the Windows backspace key. Most Mac keyboards don't have a Forward Delete key anymore, though larger ones do—it's called "Del->". If you don't see it, you still can use forward delete by hitting the FN button (button left corner of your keyboard) and Delete button.

Magic Mouse / Trackpad

Aside from the already mentioned right clicking (or lack thereof), Windows and Mac mouses work about the same.

The mouse and trackpad are both missing the scroll button typically found on a Windows mouse. To scroll up and down or side to side, just move two fingers up and down or left and right. It's basically the same way you scroll on an iPhone or iPad except that you use two fingers instead of one.

The biggest difference between a Windows and Mac mouse is that a Mac mouse use something called Gestures. These can all be customized by going to "System Preferences" and "Mouse" or "Trackpad" but below is an overview of default gestures.

Note: Some of these gestures only work with a Magic Trackpad—not a Magic Mouse.

- Tap with three fingers on a word - brings up a dictionary of that word (note: does not work in all programs).
- Right Click - Click with two fingers.
- Zoom in or out - Pinch with two fingers (does not work on all programs)
- Smart Zoom (automatically zooms in) - Double tap with two fingers (does not work with all programs)
- Rotate - Rotate with two fingers (does not work with all programs)
- Swipe between two pages - scroll left or right with two fingers.

- Toggle between full-screen apps - swipe left or right with four fingers
- Bring up Notification Center - Swipe left from the right edge of your mouse with two fingers.
- Bring up Mission Control - Swipe up with three fingers.
- App Expose - Swipe down with three fingers.
- Bring up Launchpad apps - Pinch with thumb and three fingers.
- Show the desktop - Spread with your thumb and three fingers.

One minor, but helpful, feature of OS X is making it easy to find your mouse; when you move your mouse quickly, it will grow larger to help you find where it is on the screen.

Force Touch

If you have the latest MacBook (anything newer than March 2015—but not the MacBook Air) then you will have a brand new feature called Force Touch; Force Touch is something you'll soon see on all iPhones, iPads and pretty much every new Apple device—it's actually already on the Apple Watch. So what is it? It measures how much pressure you are giving the trackpad—if you tap down on your trackpad over an icon or image, and then press all the way, it will show you a preview of it.

On iPhone's this feature is called "3D Touch"; it's a little different, but it's basically the same.

You can change your Force Touch settings by going into System Preference and Mouse / Trackpad.

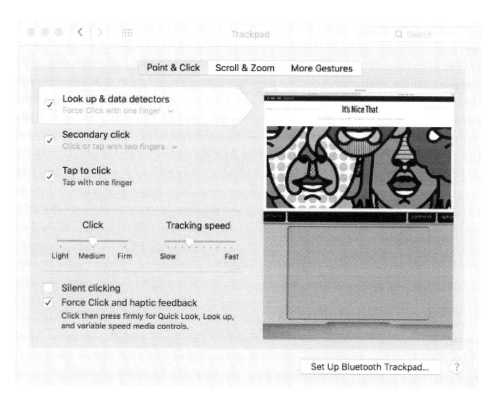

You'll notice when you push down on your trackpad, it feels like it's clicking twice; when your computer is off, it won't feel like that because you need the computer powered on for the force feedback to work.

Here's a brief overview of some of the things you can do with Force Touch; as you use your Mac, you'll discover dozens and dozens more—especially as developers begin to implement it in software.

- Look up: Force click text in a webpage and a popover appears, showing you Look up results for that text. It may be a dictionary, Wikipedia page or something else.
- Addresses: Force click an address to see a Maps preview of that location.
- Events: Force click dates and events to add them to Calendar.
- Link previews: Force click a link in Safari or Mail to see an inline preview of the webpage.
- File icons: Force click a file icon to see a Quick Look preview of the file's content.
- File names: Force click a file name in the Finder or on your desktop to edit the file name.
- Dock: Force click an app icon in the Dock to access App Exposé. This shows you all open windows for that app.
- QuickTime and iMovie: You can vary the pressure you use on fast-forward and rewind buttons.
- Map zooming: Press harder on a zoom button to accelerate as you zoom in and out of a map.

The Desktop

Hopefully by now your files are transferred, you've completed the initial start up, and you have a pretty picture on your desktop. At last, you are ready to use your computer!

The desktop is where you'll be spending much of your time, so let's take some time getting to know it.

The first thing you should notice is that it's really not that much different from Windows—it's a vast space that you can either leave empty or fill with icons or documents.

Menu Bar

One of the most noticeable differences between Windows and Mac on the desktop is the top menu bar. I'll be referring back to this menu bar throughout the book, but right now what you need to know is this bar changes with each program that you open, but some of the features remain the same. The little apple, for instances, never changes—clicking on this will always bring up options to restart, shut down, or log out of your computer. The little magnifying glass at the far right is also always there. Any time you click on that, you can search for files, emails, contacts, etc. that are on your computer.

Menulets

At the top right, you'll see several "menulets," which include Bluetooth, wireless connectivity, volume, battery, time and date, the name of the account currently logged in, Spotlight, and Notifications, as well as other assorted third party icons (if installed).

As this book continues, we'll refer back to this part of the menu part.

Dock

Windows has a taskbar on the bottom of the screen, and Mac has a dock; the dock is where all your commonly used applications are.

If you see a little dot under the icon, then the program is currently open. If you want to close it, then click the icon with two fingers to bring up the options, and then click Quit.

Removing a program from the dock is pretty simple—just drag the icon to the trash and let go. This will not remove the program—it only removes the shortcut. Finder, Trash, and Launchpad are the only programs that you cannot remove.

If you want to add a program to the dock, then open it; when the icon appears on the dock, click with two fingers, then go to Options and select Keep in Dock.

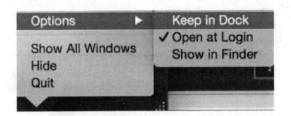

Trash

At the right end of the Dock is the Trash. To delete a folder, file or application, drag the item to the Trash, or right click the item and select Move to Trash from the pop-up menu. If you want to eject a disk or drive, such as an iPod or USB flash drive, drag the volume into the Trash. As the volume hovers over the trash, the icon morphs from a trash can to a large eject button. Release the mouse, and your volume will be safely ejected and can be removed from the computer. To empty the trash, right click (click with two fingers) on the Trash icon in the Dock, and select Empty Trash.

You can manage the trash yourself, but I also highly recommend an app called "Clean My Mac" (https://macpaw.com/cleanmymac); it's a little expensive, but when I use it, it normally helps me free up 1GB of storage just by deleting installation files and extensions that I don't need.

App Buttons

The little lights in the image above have no name. Some people call them traffic lights. You'll start seeing a lot of them because nearly all Mac programs use them. On a Windows, you've seen them as an X and a minus in the upper right of your screen. On a Mac they appear in the upper left of the running program. The red light means close, the yellow light means minimize, and the green makes the app full screen.

Full screen means the program takes up the entire screen and even the dock disappears. You can see the dock and other programs quickly by swiping the trackpad to the right with four fingers. To get back to the app, swipe with four fingers to your left.

Finder

The first icon on your dock—one of three that cannot be deleted or moved—is the Finder icon.

Finder is the Mac equivalent of Explorer on a Windows computer; as the name implies, it finds things. Finder is pretty resourceful and powerful so this section will be a little longer than others, because there's a lot you can do with it.

Let's get started on clicking on the Finder icon.

There are four ways to view folders on your Mac - icons, lists, columns and Cover Flow. Different views make sense for different file types, and you can change the view using the View Options icons (pictured above).

Cover Flow View

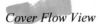

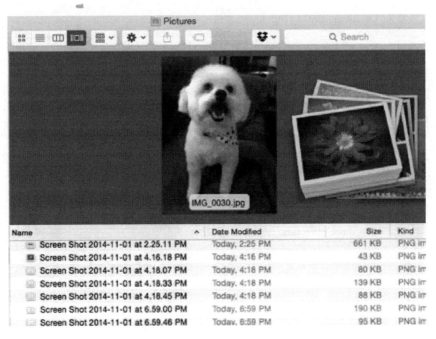

Cover Flow lets you quickly go through thumbnails / previews of photos (it's a little like Film Strip in Windows); you can also sort any of the columns by clicking on the header—so if you are looking for a larger file, then click the Size column or if you are looking for a recent file, then pick the Date Modified column.

Icon View

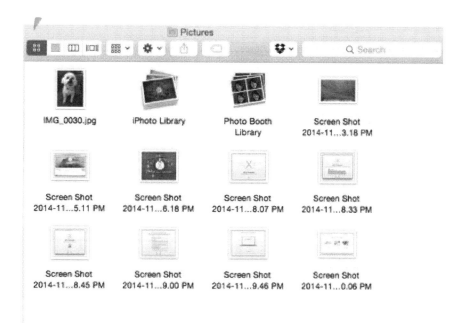

Icon View can help if you need to sort through several image files or applications. It gives you either a thumbnail of each picture or an icon for each file or app.

List View

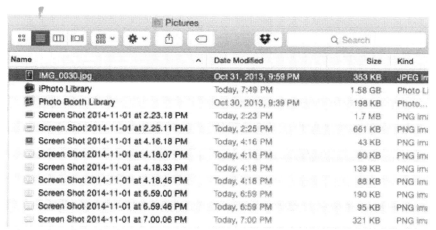

List View, on the other hand, gives you more information about the file, including the date it was last modified. This is the perfect view for sorting.

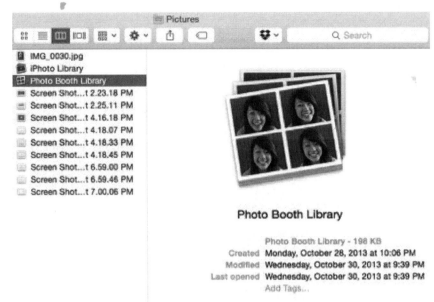

Finally, Column View which is kind of a hybrid of List View and Cover Flow View. It shows the folder hierarchy a file is located in. Notice that Finder doesn't include the Windows "go up one level" button – Column View is a good way to get the same results and navigate easily through your file structure.

Sorting in Finder

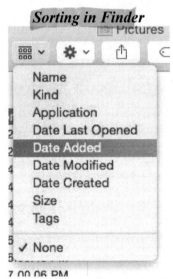

Finder gives you a number of ways to sort your files and folders. You can sort by name, type, application required for opening the file (like Microsoft Word, for example), the date the file was created, modified, or opened, the file size, and any tags you may have applied.

File Management

Most file management tasks in OS X are similar to Windows. Files can be dragged and dropped, copied, cut and pasted. If you need to create a new folder, use the Gear icon in Finder, which will give you the option you need.

Sierra also allows you to batch rename files (i.e. rename several files at once instead of one at a time), potentially saving you hours of time, depending on your file system. To take advantage of this, select the files you'd like to rename (hint: use COMMAND + click to select multiple files, or use COMMAND + A to select everything). Then right-click the selected files and choose "Rename X items."

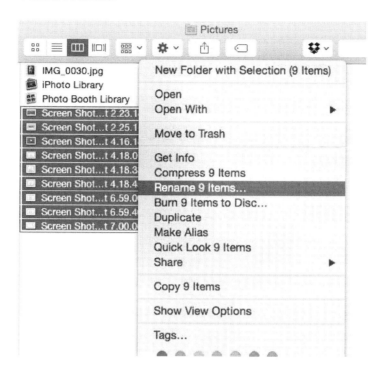

You'll then have the option to replace text or to add text to the file names.

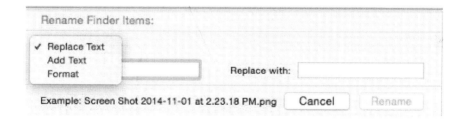

Favorites

If you look on the left side of the Finder Window, you'll see a Favorites sidebar. This section includes high-frequency folders, like Documents, Pictures, Downloads, and more.

To add an application or file to your Favorites menu, just drag it over to the Favorites area and drop it. To remove an item from Favorites, right-click it (click with two fingers) and select Remove From Sidebar.

Tabbed Browsing

Apple took a page from Internet browsers by adding something called "Tabbed Browsing" to Finder. Basically instead of having several Finder boxes open (which is how you had to do it in older OS') you open tabs. To open an additional Finder tab, press COMMAND+t or click File and New Tab.

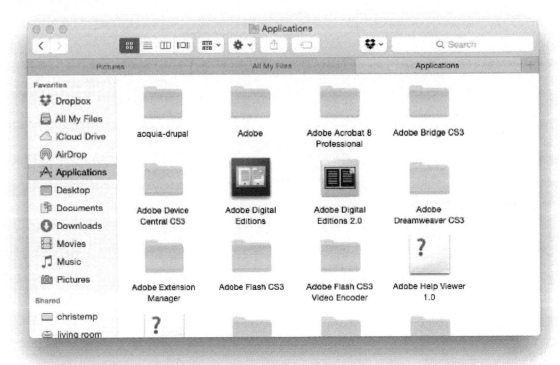

If you want to merge all of your tabbed windows, just click Windows in the file menu on the top of your screen, and then Merge All Windows.

Tags

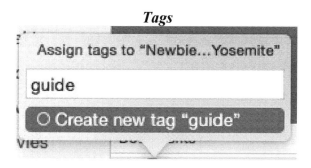

If you use photo apps like Flickr, then you probably know all about tagging; it's essentially adding subjects to your file to make it easier to find. Let's say the file is regarding the 2015 tax year—you can add a tag to the file called "2015 Taxes" or whatever you want it to be. You can also color code it.

To assign a tag to a file (you can also assign it to a folder), click the file / folder with two fingers, and then click tags; if this is your first take just type it in and hit Enter; if you've already tagged a file and want to use the same name, then click the name of the tag as it appears.

Launchpad

Launchpad is essentially the Start menu on a Windows computer. It shows your programs.

When you click it, you'll see rows of programs; you can immediately start typing to search for an app, or you can just look for it. If you have a lot of apps, then you probably have more than one screen. Swipe with two fingers to the left to see the next screen.

Launchpad takes a lot of cues from iPhone and iPad. If you want to remove a program, for example, you do it the same way you remove an iPhone or iPad app. Just click and hold until an X appears above it, then click the X to remove it. Similarly, to rearrange icons, use the same method for rearranging iPhone / iPad apps—click and hold over the icon until it begins to shake, and then move it wherever you want it to go. You can even put programs into groups the same way as an iPhone / iPad—click and hold over the icon, then drag it on top of the app you want to group it with; finally, when the folder appears, you can let go.

After you delete a program, you can re-download it anytime, by going into the app store (as long as you downloaded it from the app store and not from a website).

Notifications

For the past few updates, Apple has attempted to replicate iOS (iPad / iPhone) features; the move is meant to make using a Mac much like using a mobile device. This attempt at replicating features is especially true with Sierra OS.

Notifications is a new feature to OS X Yosemite. You can find it on the top menu button at all times; it's to the far right hand corner and looks like this:

Click it any time you want to see alerts. You can also access it by swiping with two fingers to the left from the edge of your trackpad.

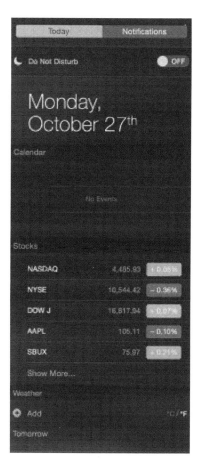

When you swipe down from the top of an iPad or iPhone you will get a similar screen. There are two parts of the Notifications menu: Today and Notifications.

The Today tab is where you'll see things happening more in the moment—what's the weather, what's in your calendar, what's going on with your stocks, etc. The Notifications tab is where you'll see things like Facebook messages or emails. Later in this book, I'll show you how to customize it.

Split View

Split view is perhaps the biggest added feature to OS X. It let's you run two apps side-by-side—but there's a catch: not all apps are compatible. So if your scratching your head because this feature won't work for you, then chances are it's not that you are doing it wrong—it's that the app doesn't support the feature.

There are two ways to get split view to work. Let's look at both of them. First make sure the two apps that you want to run side-by-side are not running in full-screen mode.

Method 1

Click and hold the green button in the upper left corner of your app.

A transparent blue box will appear; drag and drop the app into it (by default, the blue is on the left side, but if you drag to the right side, it will also turn blue and you can drop it in).

Next, click the program you want to use side-by-side.

A side-by-side window now appears; you can use the middle black line to make one bigger or smaller, by dragging left or right.

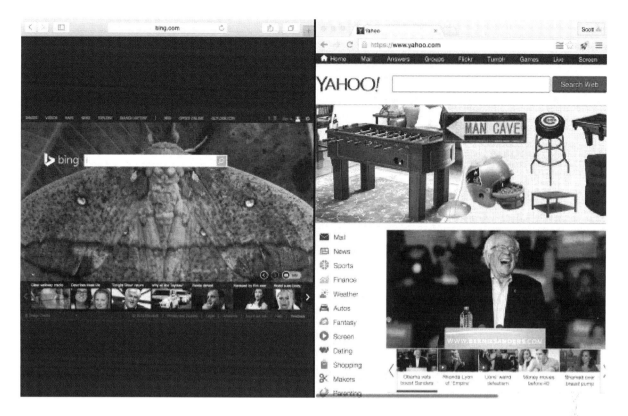

To return to the normal view, click the green button in the upper left corner of the app once more (you can also hit the ESC key on your keyboard).

Method 2

As you are probably noticing, most things in OS X can happen by several different methods; side-by-side view has two. The second way to get apps is to open your Mission Control , and drag the app to the top menu.

You'll notice, a grey box appear and the box appears to split.

Desktop 1

Once you drop it into that box, you'll see a side-by-side preview. Once you click the preview, it will maximize.

Safari & Google Chrome

Returning to the non-split screen is done the same way as method 1 (click the green box in the upper left corner or hit the ESC key on the keyboard)

Tabbed Software

If you've ever used Tabs on Internet Explorer or Chorme, then this next feature might interest you. It allows you to open documents (such as Maps and Pages) with tab viewing. NOTE: not all Mac App support this feature.

To use it, open two windows of the same app. I'll use Maps in the example below.

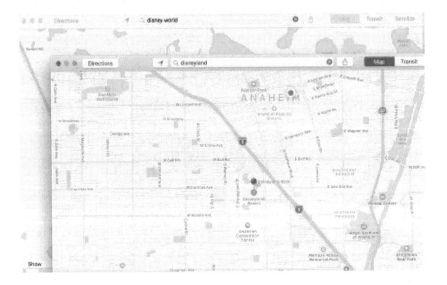

Next, go to Window and Merge All Windows.

Your windows should now be merged.

Internet

The Mac is a beautiful machine, but you can only admire that desktop for so long; eventually you'll want to get on the Internet, so let me explain how.

There are two methods: Ethernet (i.e. plugging in a LAN cable to your computer) and Wireless.

Setting Up With Ethernet

All new Mac computers are set up with Wi-Fi; iMacs also have Ethernet ports to plug in a network cable. This option isn't available on any of the Mac laptops—though you can buy an adaptor if you absolutely must have it.

If you have a basic Internet modem, then set up is pretty easy. Just plug a network cable into your Internet hub, and plug the other end into your Mac. Once it's plugged in, the Internet should work.

Newer Macs come with top of the line wireless radios for Wi-Fi, so you should be perfectly fine without using the Ethernet port.

Setting Up Wireless Networks

Setting up a wireless connection is also pretty simple. Just click the Wi-Fi menu on the menu bar. It looks like the image below and is near the upper right corner:

As long as there's a wireless network in range, it will show up when you click it (sometimes it does take a few seconds to appear).

If there's a lock next to the Wi-Fi name, then you'll need to know the passcode (if it's a home Internet connection, then it's usually on the bottom of your Internet modem; if it's at a business, then you'll have to ask for the code. If there's no lock, then it's an open network. You usually see this kind of network at places like Starbucks.

If it's a locked network, then as soon as you click on it, it will ask for the code; once it's entered and you click Connect, then you're connected (assuming you added it right); if it's not locked then once you click on it, then it will attempt to connect.

If you own one of the above-mentioned computers, or would rather connect to a network wirelessly, you can do it by clicking on the Wi-Fi menulet in the top menu bar.

Airport Express / Airport Extreme

If you need more range in your wireless connection, or want to set up a private network, Apple sales to Mac accessories. One is the Airport Express ($99) and the other is the Airport Extreme ($199 or $299 to $399 if you'd like one with a hard drive).

The Express is a good option for people wanting to add a private network (so, for instance, you can have a network just for guest and guest printing); the Airport Extreme gives excellent range; I use one in my home because the modem supplied with my phone company could barely reach the next room over and the signal strength was weak; the Extreme not only got to the next room, but it got several more rooms—I can now get a signal more than 100 feet from where the Extreme is located. It's a pretty easy installation, and Apple has videos for those who need extra help.

The more expensive models are also a good option for backing up computers. The $299 and $399 models offer up to 3TB of storage; the way it works is your computer connects to it, and will back up your computer in the background, so your computer is always being backed up. These models also let you share files. So, for instance, if you want a private storage locker for anyone who connects to your network, then you could do so here.

Safari

Just as a Windows computer has Internet Explorer as the default web browser, Mac has Safari as the default web browser; if you've used Safari on your iPhone or iPad then you should already be accustomed to using it.

Noticeably absent from Safari is something called "Flash". Flash is what you might used to watch some videos and other web apps; you can always download it, but this will affect the battery life of your laptop, as Flash tends to drain the battery quickly—which is one of the reasons Apple does not include it.

You are also free to download other Internet browsers. Some of the popular free ones are Google Chrome (www.google.com/chrome/), Mozilla Firefox (www.mozilla.org/firefox), and Opera (www.opera.com).

One of the biggest advantages of using Safari over another web browser is a feature called Handoff. Let's say you're reading an article on your phone on the subway coming into work; you get to work and want to pick up where you left off on a larger Mac screen; just open up Safari, then click the two square boxes in the upper right corner.

If your iPhone or iPad is synced with the computer, then you'll see its name and pages that it's currently browsing. You can also handoff a Mac page to your iPhone or iPad in the same way.

In addition to websites, handoff also lets you seamlessly sync things like maps, messages, and documents (Pages, Numbers, and Presentation documents).

Mail

Mail is the Mac equivalent of Outlook; like Safari, it works in a very similar way to iPad and iPhone. Apple will provide you with a free email address that ends @icloud.com, but you can also add normal email into the application (like Hotmail, Yahoo, and Gmail).

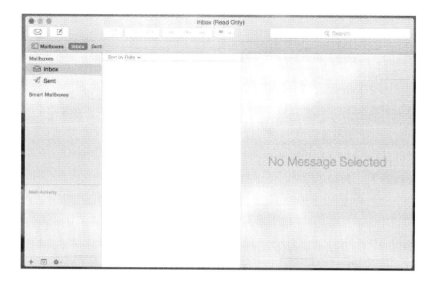

Adding Accounts

To get started, you need to add your email account. Locate the Mail app by clicking on Launchpad, and then clicking the Mail app icon.

Once the app opens, go to the top menu bar and click Mail > Add Account. This will load the Add Account dialogue box.

Select the provider that you will be adding in (Note: you can go back and add as many accounts as you want) and click Continue. Next you'll be asked what your Name, Email Address, and Password is.

If you are using a popular email provider, set up is pretty self-explanatory. If you are using a business email, then you will probably need to work with your system administrator to get it added in correctly.

Once it's set up, you should start seeing mail show up on your computer.

Sending an Email

Now that you have an account added, you can start sending mail; to send mail you can either press Command+N on your keyboard, go to the top menu and select File and New Message, or click the Compose icon (it looks like a pencil going through a square).

The New Message dialogue box will appear. In the To field, enter the email address or addresses that you'd like to send a message to, add in a subject and message, and then hit the paper airplane in the upper left corner when you are ready to send the message.

You can also add formatting to the message by clicking on the "A" button. Formatting is very basic—you can bold, add italics, underline, and change the coloring.

Contacts

Unless you are a business person, having contacts on your computer might not seem necessary; here's the advantage of it—it syncs with your phone. So having a contact on your computer will carry over to your other mobile devices. To use it, go to your Launchpad, then click the icon.

If you're signed into iCloud, then you should see dozens of contacts already. To create a new contact, click on the (+) button at the bottom of the main window. On the next screen add all the info you want—it can be as much or as little as you desire. Some contacts may only need a website address, others might have mailing address—it's entirely up to you how much information you add. You can also edit a contact by finding their name, then clicking on the Edit button. If you want to delete someone, then find their name and hit Delete on your keyboard (you can also delete by clicking on their name with two fingers).

Picture-In-Picture Video

If you'd like to watch a video while you work, then you're in luck! If you already own the video (a video you purchased on iTunes, for example), then just start playing the video and go to View and Float on Top.

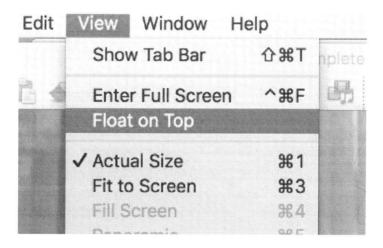

But what about Web videos? Such as Vimeo and YouTube? That's easy too. Just double click the video you are watching, and select Enter Picture-In-Picture.

Your video will immediately begin playing above other windows.

Apple products really work best with other Apple products; that's even truer with Sierra, where you can sync your iPhone account to make phone calls (both video and regular) and send messages right from your Mac. Additionally, you can even use your iPhone's data connection to get Internet on your laptop on the go—this is especially handy while travelling if you don't want to pay for Wi-Fi spots that charge for access (just keep in mind that your data connection does have monthly limits and using a computer can go through those limits very quickly—in other words, this probably isn't something you want to do to stream Netflix movies).

iMessage

When you use iMessages from your Mac to send messages, just keep in mind that it's kind of like instant messaging for Mac users—that means it's designed to work with Mac products…nothing else.

Setting Up iMessage
1. To set up iMessage, click the Messages icon to launch it.
2. If you were already logged into iCloud on the Mac, you will automatically be logged into iMessage.
3. If you'd like to change this account or haven't yet logged in, select Messages > Preferences on the top menu bar.
4. When the Accounts dialogue box comes up, click on the Accounts tab.
5. In the left hand window, you will see iMessage. Select it.
6. The following screen will prompt you to enter the email address and password associated with iCloud. Do so and click the blue Sign In button to complete the setup process.

Setting Up Other IM Clients

While iMessage is made for Mac products, you can use it for other messaging servers like Google, Yahoo, and AOL. To add other instant messaging (IM) clients to Messages:

1. Open up Messages if it isn't already running.
2. On the top menu bar, click Messages > Add Account.

3. Select the type of account that you'd like to add, such as Gmail or Yahoo, and select Continue.
4. You will be prompted to enter the appropriate email address and password, and click the Set Up button to finish.

So now that it's set up, how do you send a message?

Start New Conversation
1. Before we begin, take a look at the entire Messages screen. It should be totally empty with no conversations. On the left sidebar it will say No Conversations. This is where you will be able to change between different conversations with people by clicking on each one. On the right hand side, you will also see No Conversation Selected. Here is where you will be able to type new messages and read everything in whatever conversation is currently selected. If you have an iPhone (or any phone for that matter), it will be like the screen where you read your text messages.
2. To create a new conversation with someone, click the Compose new message button located at the top of the left sidebar, next to the search bar. It should look a little pencil inside of a square.

When you get a message, if your sound is enabled, you'll get a little chime.

Tapbacks

If you've used Stickers on the iPad and iPhone, you might be disappointed to see that feature has not yet arrived on Mac OS. There is one feature from iOS: Tapbacks. Tapbacks let you respond to a message to indicate you like what the message says or that you agree with it. To use it, right click on any message and select your response.

FaceTime

FaceTime allows you to connect with friends and family using your computer's built-in camera. I've heard people say they are worried that someone is watching them through their webcam that they cover it with tape. When FaceTime is in use (i.e. when the camera is on and people can see you) a bright green light comes on—so you don't have to worry about people spying on you...if you don't see the light, then the camera is off.

The app can be launched by clicking on Launchpad > FaceTime.

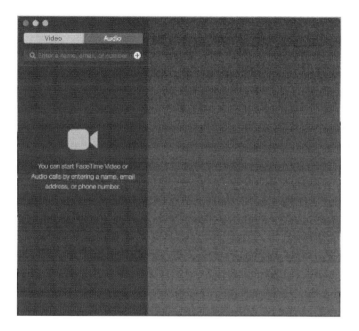

On the left side you can enter a person's name if they are in your Contacts, or a phone number. For FaceTime to work, the other person must also have an Apple device, and accept your call.

You can also use FaceTime audio. This lets you call someone without the camera—it's essentially a Wi-Fi phone call.

Photo Booth

We're a culture of selfies, so it's appropriate to talk about the app that takes your picture.

To get started, go to Launchpad and click the Photo Booth icon.

Couple of things you should notice once the app loads. First, you! If you look to the top of your screen, there should be a green light. That tells you the camera is on. But now click on a different app in your Dock—see how the green light goes off? And now click on the Photo Booth icon again, and once again the green light is on. What's going on with that light? The light indicates your camera is on—but it only stays on while you are in the Photo Booth app.

Are you ready to take a picture? Put on your silly face and click the camera button.

Like a lot of Apple apps, it's a powerful app with not a lot to it. There are only a handful of options. So let's talk about those options.

First, like a lot of Mac apps, this one can be run in full screen mode; just click the green button in the upper left corner. To exit full screen mode, you can either click the green button again or hit the ESC button on your keyboard. When you are using an app in full screen, you can always get back to your desktop by swiping with three fingers to your right on the trackpad.

So that first photo was just for fun and now you want to get rid of it. That's really easy; on the bottom of the screen you'll see all of your recent photos. Click the one you want to delete, and hit the X in the corner.

But let's say you really like a photo—so much so that you want to share it with all of your friends. Just click the photo, and then hit the square button with an arrow pointing up, and pick how you want to share it.

There are all sorts of effects for taking photos and videos. Try a few out; just click on the Effects button in the bottom right corner (NOTE: if you don't see that button then you probably are still viewing your photos, so click the camera button to get back).

Effects

This will bring up 45 different camera effects.

You won't see all 45 at once; you'll see them 9 at a time; click arrows or the circles to see the next nine effects (NOTE: The last page of effects is for you to add your own backgrounds). When you see the effect you want, just click it.

When you are back to the main screen, there are three options in the lower left corner of the box.

The default box is the middle one. That takes one photo. The first one will take four different photos (one in each box), and the last will take a video of you. When using the video option, the camera will change to a video recorder.

If you want to use some of the fancier effects where it puts you somewhere you aren't (say Yosemite or the beach), then it will ask you to step out of the picture so it can detect the background; then after a few seconds you will step back in. It's best to use a solid background for this effect. If you aren't happy with the way it looks, then you can reset the filter by going to the Menu bar on top, then clicking View and finally clicking Reset effect.

View	Camera	Window	Help

Show Photo ⌘1
Show Effects ⌘2
Show Last Effect ⌘3

Next Page of Effects ⌘→
Previous Page of Effects ⌘←

Reset Effect ⇧⌘R

Start Slideshow
Enter Full Screen ^⌘F

If you want to add your own background, then go to the last page of Effects, and drag a photo of your choice into the box. Once you see that photo appear, click on it to activate the effect.

Don't be afraid to play around with the program. There's nothing you can press that will mess anything up!

Calendar

Calendar is another feature that can be synced to your iCloud account—so as long as you're using the same account, then everything you put in your calendar from your computer will also show up on your iPhone and iPad. You can also sync the calendar to other ones you may be using online like Google or Yahoo.

To get started with it, go to your Launchpad in the Dock and click on the Calendar icon.

At the top of the application window from left to right you have the standard stoplight buttons, Calendars, New Event (+), several different views including Day and Month, and the Search bar.

Syncing Calendars
If you already use a calendar with iCloud, Google, Yahoo, or any other provider, you can sync it up with the Mac Calendar application.

1. In the top menu bar click Calendar > Add Account.

2. Like you did with Mail, you'll be prompted to enter your name, email address, and password.

Once you finish the setup process your events from that calendar should automatically populate in the Calendar window. If you have multiple accounts with separate calendars, you can filter through them by clicking on the Calendars button in the toolbar, and checking or unchecking the boxes next to the appropriate calendars.

Changing Views
You can change the calendar view between Day, Week, Month, or Year by clicking on the corresponding button in the toolbar.

Day will display all of that day's events, broken down by hour.

Week will show you the whole week at a glance, and display blocks for events so you can easily see when you have events, and if you have any upcoming free time.

The Month view will probably be your default view if you just need your calendar to remind you about bill payments and due dates, or don't have too many appointments each month but they are scattered through the month.

Reminders

As the name implies, the Reminders application is used to remind you of things—and, as you might have guessed by now, it can be synced using iCloud to the Reminders app on your iPhone or iPad.

The app lets you create list for things like groceries or anything else on your mind; you can also use the app to schedule when things are do—like paying a bill by the 15th of the month; it can even be set to remind you every time you leave or arrive at your home to turn your home alarm on or off.

To get started, open the app by clicking on the Launchpad icon, then selecting it from the list of apps.

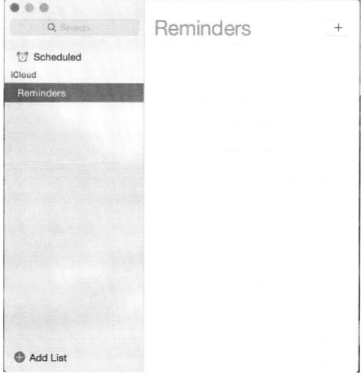

Creating Single Reminders

If you just need to be reminded of a single item, or several unrelated items, you should enter them into the Reminders list.

1. With the application open, click on Reminders in the left hand window.

2. In the main window, click on the (+) button next to the title of the list ("Reminders" in this case).

3. A new item will be added that you should name immediately. Notice the radio button that appears next to the newly-created item.

4. Once the item is named, double click on it to open up the information pane.

5. Here you'll be able to set the reminder date and time, priority level, and if you'd like to be reminded as you are arriving or leaving someplace.

6. Fast forward to the day of the reminder; once you have completed the task, you can click on the radio button next to the item to mark it as Completed.

7. You'll then be able to hide or show any previously completed items.

8. To delete items whether complete or incomplete, click on the name to highlight it and press the Delete key.

Creating New Lists

Single list are great for things like "open the gate Monday for the gardener" or "Pay the utility bill on Tuesday" but if you want to create reminders for things like shopping lists, then you'll need to create a reminder list—these can be as long (or short) as you want.

1. Open up the Reminders application if you closed out of it before.

2. On the left hand side of the window, at the bottom you will see (+) Add List. Click it and enter a name for your newly-created list.

3. Once the new list is named, click on it and press the (+) button next to the list title as you did with Reminders to add new items. You can also choose whether you want due dates or not.

Location Based Reminder

If you want to create a reminder that is location based (i.e. "when I leave work, remind me to call wife") then follow the steps above.

Click the Information icon next to the reminder (the "i" with a circle)

This will bring up a few extra options. One says, "remind me" with a checkbox for "At a location"; click that checkbox. Next, enter the address, and select if you want the reminder when you get there or when you're leaving there.

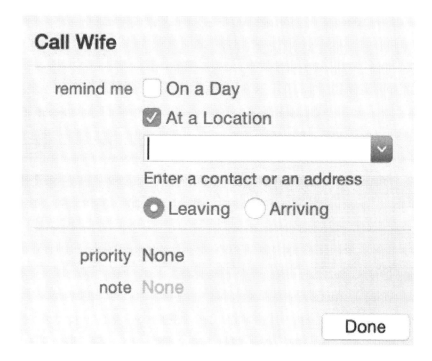

Notes

Newer Macs come with Pages preinstalled, so what's the point of notes? Notes is a more basic program than Pages or Word—you can't do any fancy formatting. The advantage is that it opens and saves quickly. So in short, Notes is for when you just need to jot something down quickly.

To open it, go to the Launchpad icon on your Dock and click the Notes icon.

Notes, like most of the apps in Sierra, syncs to your iPhone and iPad as long as you are logged into the same iCloud account.

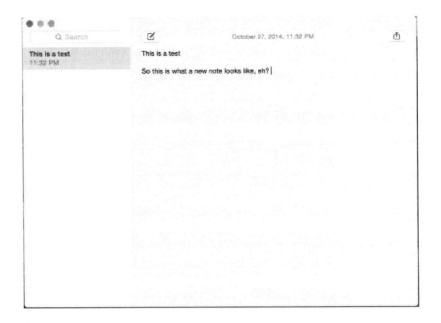

Creating and Editing Notes

1. There are a few different ways to create a brand new note. You can start a new note by clicking on the Compose icon (the square with a pencil going through it), or double clicking an empty space in the left sidebar. You can also right-click the left sidebar and select New Note.
2. Once the note is created, the line will begin blinking in the right window, indicating that it's time for you to get writing.
3. The notes will automatically save as you type, so exiting Notes won't mean you lose progress.
4. If you need to pick up where you left off on a note, you can use the search bar to find the exact note you are looking for, or scroll through the left sidebar and select the appropriate note. With the note highlighted, click anywhere in the right window to begin editing that note, or double-click to open up a smaller window.
5. To remove notes, find the one you'd like to delete and highlight it. Press the Delete key and confirm it. You can also right-click a note and select Delete.

Notes can be shared through different outlets like LinkedIn, Facebook, Mail, and Messages. If you'd like to share a note, click on the Share button in the top right corner and select how you'd like to send it.

iTunes

You probably know what iTunes is; you might even use it. On a Mac it's really not that different from a Windows computer; the main difference is that on a Windows computer music is played through the Windows Media Player by default and on a Mac, it's played on iTunes.

Keep in mind that you should use the same iTunes account on your Mac that you use on other devices because the media you buy on iTunes will show up on all of your devices. The exception is rentals—rentals are only available on the device you buy it from. So if you rent something on your Mac, don't expect to be able to watch it on your Apple TV or iPad; this is a studio licensing issue, not an Apple one. You do, however, have the option of using AirPlay for rentals to send it to your Apple TV.

Adding Music to your Library

This section is for adding music you already own and have on the computer. If you don't have any music, you should probably skip ahead to the iTunes Store section first.

1. At the top menu bar, click File > Add to Library.
2. When the window comes up, use the left bars to search for the specific song or songs that you'd like to add.
3. If you already have a giant music collection that you may have carried over from an old computer, you can import entire folders all at once.
4. When you've decided what to add, click on it once to highlight it, and select the blue Open button.
5. It may take some time depending on how many songs you are importing, but iTunes will show you the progress.
6. Once complete, click on the My Music tab again to verify that your music has been added to the iTunes collection.

Playlists

The Playlists section is where you can view, edit and delete playlists you may have created. On the left hand side you will notice that Apple has created some for you: 90's Music, Classical Music, My Top Rated, Recently Added, Recently Played, and Top 25 Most Played. These are pretty self-explanatory, and Apple uses a song's built-in metadata to determine which songs will fit in those premade playlists.

At the top of the list you will also see one called Genius. Selecting Genius will allow you to use Apple's specially made music mixer. It takes songs from your music collection and creates great-sounding custom playlists and mixes.

Using Genius

If this is the first time you are using Genius, you will have to first click on the button that says Turn On Genius.

Once you turn it on, there will be three steps that happen automatically. Depending on the size of your library, this may take awhile so grab a snack. Once it's finished, your computer screen will greet you with a message that says Genius has been successfully turned on.

Match

iTunes Match is great if you have a large music library but don't have enough storage on your phone. Signing up for Match will allow you to store your entire collection on iCloud, including music that you've ripped from CDs and didn't purchase through iTunes. This way you'll be able to stream your entire library from any Apple device connected to iCloud without taking up any storage.

The songs are "matched" by Apple's online music database, so when you are playing the song on your iPhone, for example, it isn't actually the same file that you uploaded or purchased. Rather, it's Apple's version of the song in full 256 Kbps, even if the song you originally uploaded or purchased was of lower audio quality. If the song is not found on Apple's own servers (your cousin's Whitesnake cover band perhaps), it will playback the original file you uploaded, with the original audio quality.

Unfortunately, iTunes Match isn't free. If you'd like to sign up for it, expect to pay $24.99 for a yearly subscription. Signing up for Match does have another perk though – if you enjoy using iTunes Radio but can't stand the ads, purchasing the yearly Match subscription will remove ads from Radio.

Radio

Radio is a free music streaming service by the music lovers at Apple. Based on several different factors, Apple creates radio stations that you will probably enjoy. As you listen to different things, the stations will become more and more personalized, playing songs that are more in line with what you've been recently listening to and avoiding the ones you haven't played.

If you would like to explore the radio a little more, you can browse through artist-curated playlists created with a specific goal in mind, or just search by genre. You may also find First Plays, which allows you to listen to entire albums before buying them. This feature only works on select albums, however, so don't expect to find every album available for First Play.

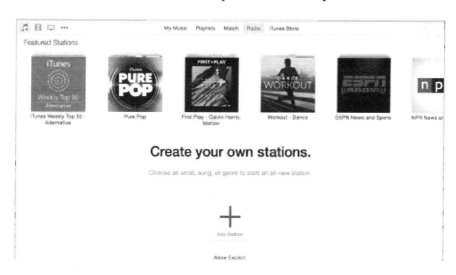

Creating a Radio Station

1. To play a new radio station, open up iTunes and click on the Radio tab.
2. If this is the first time you've used Radio, you will have to click on the blue button that says Start Listening.

3. When Radio fully loads, you will notice that the top half of the window is filled with premade radio stations like Smooth Jazz, Classic Rock, iTunes Weekly Top 50 Dance, or Pepsi Pulse Pop if you like listening to bubbly pop backed by a giant soda company. Clicking on one will automatically start playing that radio station. At the bottom of the screen you can also toggle explicit language on or off.
4. If these stations just aren't cutting it, you can create your own by clicking the gigantic + button that says Add Station.
5. You can choose a genre as a starting point; or, if you'd like to be more specific, use the Search bar to enter the name of an artist, song, or genre that you'd like to listen to. The results will be similar music to what you originally searched for.
6. The station will begin playing and you can see the track information at the top of iTunes, but the main difference with Radio is that since you don't already own the music, you'll be able to see how much it would cost to buy the song currently playing.

iTunes Store

If you don't own any music yet and are looking to build a digital song collection, or if you own music but would like to add new tracks, the iTunes store is where you can browse, purchase and download new music. In addition to music you can also buy movies, TV shows, podcasts, audiobooks, and books.

Clicking on the Search bar in the top right-hand corner will pull up trending searches in case you are looking for what's hot. If you are looking for a specific song or movie, type it into the Search bar and iTunes will load it for you. Scroll through the main page and the latest releases will be shown front and center, letting you see new music at a glance.

On the right side of the screen you will see Music in big letters, with All Genres under it. Clicking the All Genres link opens a dropdown menu with every main genre you can think of.

The big Music link will open a dropdown menu with the rest of the iTunes store options: Movies, TV shows, App Store, Books, Podcasts, Audiobooks, and iTunes U. Go through each one and you will see that they all follow the same conventions as the Music page, with charts, top downloads, and new releases.

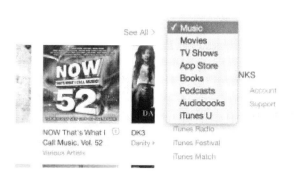

To purchase new music (or any other media) that interests you, use either the search bar or browse through the categories to find what you're looking for. When you reach a song or album you'd like, click it to bring up the full information menu for that item.

The window will display all types of information including album price, individual song price, track list, audio previews, release date, ratings, reviews, and similar items. To buy the album (or a single song), click on the price; a prompt window will come up to make sure you really wanted to buy that album, and you can continue by clicking the blue Buy button.

If you already have funds in your iTunes account, or have a card on file, the purchase will be made and the song(s) will begin to automatically download. If you don't have any money in the account, or haven't yet added a payment method, you will be asked to enter that information before the purchase can be made.

After your purchases are fully downloaded, you'll be able to enjoy your new music by clicking on the My Music tab and selecting your latest addition.

App Store

The App Store is where you'll be able to download and install many different applications that have been developed specifically for use with a Mac computer. These apps will do everything from add new functionalities and make your life easier, to providing a fun way to waste time and play some games during downtime at work. Keep in mind that for the App Store to be functional, you need to be connected to the Internet.

To be clear, Apps purchased on the App Store *only* run on Macs; if you have two Macs, you can download it on both if you have the same account. But you cannot download them on your iPhone or iPad. So if you are wondering why a game you downloaded on the iPhone or iPad is not available free on your Mac, that's why. Mac Apps are developed using an entirely different framework.

Open the App Store by selecting it either through the dock or Launchpad. The App Store's home page will greet you, showing you the latest and greatest in the world of apps.

At the top you will see different sections: Featured, Top Charts, Categories, Purchases, and Updates.

The Featured, Top Charts, and Categories tabs will show you apps that can be downloaded, but organized in different ways. Featured will show you Best New Apps, Best New Games, Editor's Choices, and collections of different apps that work great together.

Top Charts shows you the best of the best when it comes to available apps, and is broken down by Top Paid, Top Free, and Top Grossing. On the right side, you can also browse through Top Apps broken down by category, in case you wanted to refine your search.

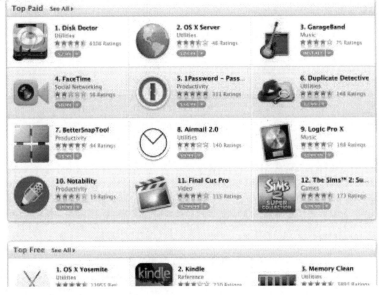

Categories further breaks down your app hunting into different categories like Business, Education, Reference, Productivity, Medical, Entertainment, and Games.

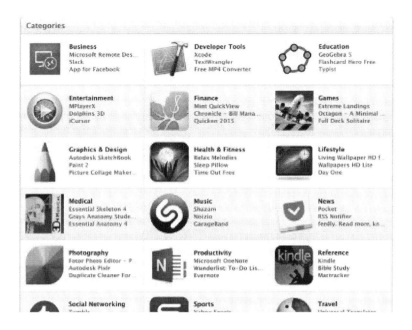

Choosing a category will bring up more selections and the right side will be filled with even more categories. For example, selecting the Business category will bring you to the main Business apps page where the hottest apps are listed. On the right side, smaller categories like Apps for Writers, App Development, or Apps for Designers can be selected. It doesn't matter what category of apps you are currently under; the list remains the same in the right half.

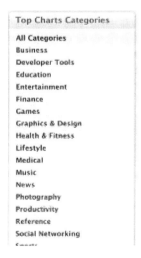

Purchases and Updates are where you can go to view past App Store downloads. The Purchases title can be a bit misleading, because your free apps will also appear here. In the Updates section, you can view which apps need to be updated to the latest version. If you have multiple apps that need updating, you can choose the Update All button and it will go down the entire list.

Lesser Used Apps

There are a lot of apps on Mac that you probably see but don't use. Here's a rundown of some of those apps and when you might use them.

TextEdit is Apple's answer to Microsoft's Notepad. This is a simple plain text editor. It's certainly not fancy, but it's good for jotting down notes.

Stickies is a love it or hate it sort of app. If you're in the love it camp, though, they're still there. Stickies are like Post-it notes for your desktop. Just open the Stickies app from Launchpad and start sticking away!

Make a note of it!

Stickies lets you keep notes (like these) on your desktop. Use a Stickies note to jot down reminders, lists, or other information. You can also use notes to store frequently used text or graphics.

• To close this note, click the close button.

• To collapse this note, double click the title bar.

Your current notes appear when you open Stickies.

Family Sharing

Before finishing this section, I want to talk about one last feature that's not part of Sierra—it's part of Apple products in general. It's called Family Sharing. With Family Sharing, you can set up one account for everyone in your house, but everyone has separate user names. This means if someone buys a movie, song, app, etc, then everyone in your family plan can access it. But don't think you can share this with your friends…well you could, but it's not recommended because whenever they buy something, your credit card is charged—it also would break the terms and conditions you are agreeing to.

To enable Family Sharing, go to System Preferences > iCloud. Then, click Set Up Family Sharing to get started. The person who initiates Family Sharing for a family is known as the family organizer. It's an important role, since every purchase made by other family members will be made using the family organizer's credit card!

Invite your family members to join Family Sharing by entering their Apple IDs. As a parent, you can create Apple IDs for your children with parental consent. When you create a new child Apple ID, it is automatically added to Family Sharing.

There are two types of accounts in Family Sharing: adult and child. As you'd expect, child accounts have more potential restrictions than adult accounts do. Of special interest is the Ask to Buy option! This prevents younger family members from running up the family organizer's credit card bill by requiring parental authorization for purchases. The family organizer can also designate other adults in the family as capable of authorizing purchases on children's devices.

Siri

If you've used Siri on the iPhone, iPad or Apple Watch, then you'll be right at home with this feature. Siri is built into the dock. To use it, just click the dock icon.

HINT: There's a shortcut key for bringing up Siri: hold the COMMAND key and Spacebar.

Siri is great for asking general questions, but it also works for doing more involved tasks. Here's a few examples of that:

Drag and Drop Images – Ask Siri to find you photos of something; it will confirm that you want web images or images on your hard drive. It will bring back photos and you can click and drag them into documents, emails, and lots of other things.

Locating Files – Siri works much like the finder…except easier. You can tell Siri to find a specific file, or you can tell Siri to find you all files opened last week, or virtually anything else.

Personal Assistant – Siri is great at doing tasks for you. You can ask Siri to email someone, read text messages, or make an appointment in your calendar. Just ask and see what happens!

If you'd like to change Siri's settings (change the voice from female to male, for example), then go to the Launchpad, open System Preferences, then click Siri.

Siri helps you get things done, just by asking. Find files on your Mac, dictate a note, check the weather, and more.

Siri

☑ Enable Siri

Language: | English (United States) | ⌄

Siri Voice: | American (Female) | ⌄

Voice Feedback: ◉ On ○ Off

Mic Input: | Internal Microphone | ⌄

Keyboard Shortcut: | Hold Command Space | ⌄

Click the Siri icon in the menu bar or in the Dock to talk to Siri. Or choose a keyboard shortcut above.

☑ Show Siri in menu bar   About Siri and Privacy   (?)

Part 2: Making the Mac Yours

So now you know the basics; you should be able to work your way around the desktop with ease and use all the basic programs comfortably. But it still doesn't feel quite...you. It still has all the default settings, colors, gestures, and backgrounds. Sure it's a cool computer, but now let's make it feel like your computer.

System Preferences

All of the main settings are accessed in System Preferences which is essentially the Mac equivalent of Control Panel on a Windows computer. So to get started, let's get to System Preferences by clicking Launchpad, then clicking the System Preferences icon.

You can also get there by clicking on the Apple in the upper left corner of the menu and clicking System Preferences.

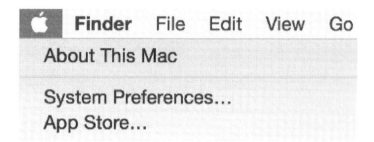

Once the app opens, you'll see there are *lots* of things that you can configure.

General

Let's get started with the first option: General. Under General, you can:

- Change the appearance of the main buttons, windows, and menus by selecting either Blue or Graphite.

- Choose the highlight color.

- Change the top menu bar and dock to dark colors. This option works well with dark wallpapers.

- Set scroll bars to display automatically based on mouse or trackpad, only when scrolling, or always on.

- Select the default web browser.

- Here is where you can allow Handoff to work between your Mac and iCloud devices (some older Macs don't support this feature).

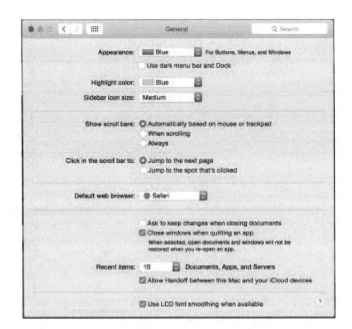

At any time, you can get back to the main System Preferences page, but clicking on either the button with 12 tiny squares. You can also hit the Back button, but if you are several menus in, you may have to hit the Back button several times.

Desktop & Screen Saver

The Desktop & Screen Saver section will help you change perhaps the most visually noticeable thing on your Mac – the desktop wallpaper. Along the left sidebar you will see several different dropdown options: Apple, iPhoto, and Folders.

At the bottom, you will be able to change the picture every so often, and you can choose how often you'd like a new image to refresh. The images that show up in the right-hand window will be the ones that get scrolled through during refreshes.

To change your desktop wallpaper to one of the great-looking images provided by Apple, or if you just want to browse the available choices, click on the Apple name. A bunch of colorful, high-resolution images will populate the right-hand side, and you can scroll through the list to find something you like. Clicking on an image will change your wallpaper to that particular selection. If you're a plain Jane and prefer to keep things really simple, you can also select Solid Colors to find an array of potentially yawn-inducing plain wallpapers.

Selecting iPhoto will let you scroll through your photos, allowing you to select a cherished memory as your wallpaper.

The Folders option will let you choose between added folders where more image files might be lying in wait. If you save lots of images to your desktop, you might want to add the Desktop folder here so you can include those images as would-be wallpapers.

Adding and Removing Folders
1. To add new folders and image collections, click on the + button located at the bottom of the left sidebar.
2. When the window comes up, search for the folder that you'd like to add.
3. Once you find the desired folder, click the blue Choose button to confirm the changes.
4. To remove a folder, highlight the folder that you'd like deleted and then click the – button to remove it.

Screen Saver

To set one up, click on the Screen Saver button at the top of the Desktop & Screen Saver window.

The left sidebar will have more options than you probably need when it comes to different ways to display your pictures. Some great ones you will probably like are Shuffling Tiles, Vintage Prints, and Classic.

On the right side you can see a preview of what your screen saver will look like. In this part of the window you can also select a source: National Geographic, Aerial, Cosmos, Nature Patterns, and Choose Folder if you have a particular folder of images you'd like to use. If you'd like to shuffle the order in which images appear, check the box next to Shuffle slide order.

At the very bottom of the window you can choose the length of time before the screen saver starts. You'll also be able to pick if you'd like to display the clock or not.

Dock

There isn't a lot you can do to the dock and most of these settings are self-explanatory. For the most part the settings just make things a little more…animated. Magnification, for example, makes an app icon larger when you hover your mouse over it.

One option I will point out, however, is the option to automatically hide and show dock; all of these settings are a matter of taste; I personally choose to hide the dock for two reasons: one, it gives you more screen space, and two, it lets you use the dock while you are in a full screen app.

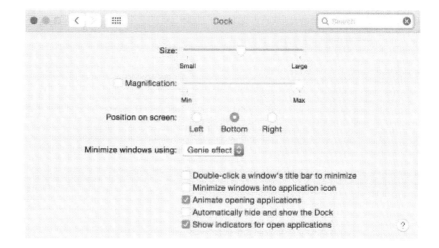

Mission Control

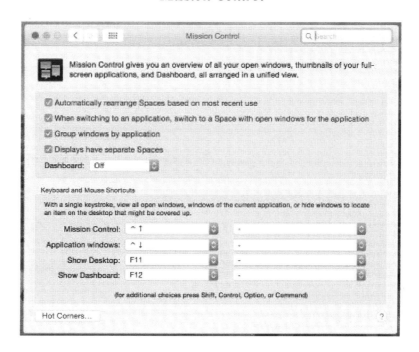

Mission Control is where you can set different parts of your screen to do different things. What do I mean by that? For example, you can set up a shortcut so that every time you move your mouse to the far upper right corner, your desktop is revealed. You can also set up shortcut keys on your keyboard. Mission Control is really about helping you make simple tasks quick.

Social Networking, Mail, Contacts and Calendars

When you use Twitter, Facebook and other apps, you may be used to just going to a website. On a Mac, you can add them into your computer's information, so you don't need to login; this also lets you get notification pop ups when you have new messages, likes, etc.

Adding Accounts

To add accounts, go to System Preferences on your Dock (the gears icon) and select Internet Accounts. From here, you can add accounts that haven't already been migrated, including iCloud, Exchange, Google, Twitter, Facebook, LinkedIn, Yahoo!, AOL, Vimeo and Flickr.

Adding accounts here will start populating Sierra's native Mail, Contacts, Reminders and Calendar apps, and add options to your Share button.

Note: You can also add accounts within the Mail, Contacts, Calendars, and Reminders apps by opening each app and clicking File > Add Account.

Twitter, Facebook, LinkedIn, Vimeo and Flickr

Sierra OS supports deep Twitter, Facebook, LinkedIn, Flickr and Vimeo integration. To get started, simply sign in to your account(s) from System Preferences > Internet Accounts. Select Twitter, Facebook, LinkedIn, Flickr, or Vimeo, and then enter your username and password. From now on, you'll be able to use that account with the Share button throughout Sierra and receive notifications in your Notifications Center.

IMG_0030.jpg

Sound

As the name implies, the Sound menu is where all changes related to sound effects and sound in general can be modified. There are three tabs that you can switch between.

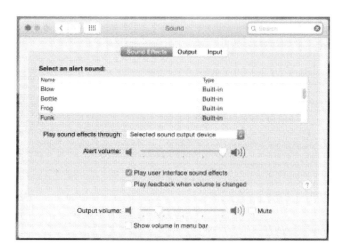

Sound Effects
The Sound Effects tab is where you can select an alert sound from the many different built-in options. By default, the following dropdown menu should be set to Selected sound output device to play the chosen sound effects through your standard speakers.

The next two checkboxes let you turn sound effects on or off for the user interface, and for volume control.

Lastly, you'll be able to adjust the output volume of your speakers. This will affect the loudness of everything from sound effects to music that's currently being played through the computer.

Input & Output
The input and output tabs are both very similar. Each will let you change the device for sound input or output (speakers or microphones), as well as adjust sound settings. In the Output tab,

you can adjust the slider to move the balance left or right, and in Input, you can change the microphone's input volume and enable or disable the built-in noise reduction feature in case you frequently use your Mac's microphone in busy cafes.

Users & Groups

If your Mac is for family use and a couple of people will be using it, then this setting will come in handy.

Along the left sidebar all existing users and groups (if you have any) will be laid out for you. To make a change to an existing user, first you need to choose the "Click the lock" icon and unlock it; unlocking lets you change settings to the user. You will also be asked for your password at this time—this is all a safety measure to ensure that if you accidentally left your computer unintended, someone couldn't come along and lock you out of your own machine.

Below are a few things you'll be able to do with each user (depending on the type of user it is admin, guest, child, etc.); some of the settings won't be available.

- Selecting the Admin user account will let you change the login password, open up the Contacts card and enable parental controls. Clicking the Login Items will allow you to change the applications that start running automatically each time you log in. There has to be at least one admin user.

- Any other created users that you make will have options to enable parental controls, change password, or turn that account into another administrator account that has full control of the Mac.

- By default you will see a Guest user set up. If it's selected, you can choose to disable the Guest user from being available as a login option. You can also set parental controls and allow guest access to your shared folders. If you do choose to keep the Guest user, keep in mind that there will be no password required, and all information and files created during that session will be deleted upon logging out.

- At the bottom of the left sidebar there is another option, called Login Options. This is where you'll find different options such as automatic login, show password hints, and show the Sleep, Shut Down, and Restart buttons. You can also display your full name or user name at the top right of the menu bar by checking the box next to Show fast user switching menu and making a selection.

Create New Users

So you know how to manage the primary user, but what about creating additional users? That's pretty simple. Just follow these steps (and make sure you have already hit that lock button to unlock the option).

1. Click on the + button.

2. From the New dropdown menu, choose from the following options: Administrator, Standard, Managed with Parental Controls, or Sharing Only.

3. Fill in the Full Name and Account Name fields. These don't have to be real names. Mickey Mouse can have a user name if you want.

4. You can choose to have the new user log in using an existing iCloud account and password, or create a whole new password.

5. If you selected Use iCloud Password, you will be prompted to enter the associated iCloud ID.

6. If you instead choose to opt for a newly-created password, you will be asked to enter it twice to verify it.

7. Once finished, click the blue Create User button. If you chose to use an iCloud ID, you will be asked to enter the password. If you made a new password, you don't need to do anything else.

Removing Existing Users

Just because you added a user, that doesn't mean they're there forever. You can delete them at anytime. But remember, deleting those deletes all the settings they've set up—so if you create again, everything will be gone.

1. To remove current users, select the user that you'd like to delete.

2. With that user highlighted, click on the – button.

3. A prompt will appear asking if you are really sure you'd like to remove the user from the computer.

4. You can also choose from one of three radio buttons: save the home folder, leave the home folder alone, or delete the home folder.

5. Once you've made a decision, click the blue Delete User button to confirm your choice and make the changes happen.

Creating Groups

If the computer is being used in a place where there are dozens of users (a classroom or library, perhaps), then creating a group would be a good option for you.

1. At the bottom of the left sidebar, click the + button.

2. From the New dropdown menu, select Group

3. In the Full Name field, create and enter a name for your group.

4. Click the blue Create Group button to confirm.

5. The new group will be created, and you will be able to check boxes next to each existing user to designate who will be a part of this group. If you have existing groups, you can also select entire groups to be a part of yet another group.

Parental Controls

If kids are using your computer, then Apple has Parental Controls to help you make sure the kids don't get into trouble. It's a pretty powerful app, but it does have a few limits—if you want ultimate protection, then there are also several paid apps like NetNanny (www.netnanny.com). Parental controls is also good for guests—if you don't mind if people use your computer, but you *only* want them to use the Internet and have no access to anything else, then you could set it up like that.

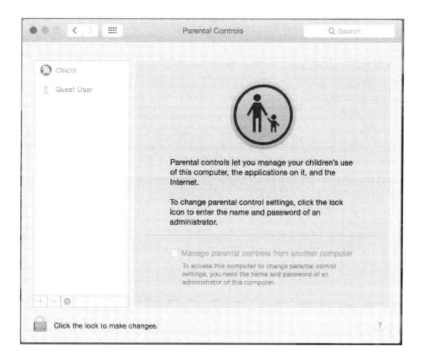

To use Apple's Parental Controls, first make sure you have created a user account for your child. Next go to System Preferences and Parental Controls.

If the padlock on the lower left corner is locked, then click it to unlock it and type in your password.

You can now set up parental controls for each child users. You can make it as restrictive as you want. The first tab lets you pick what apps they can use. You could block all apps except games, for instance. The next tab lets you control web usage. By default, Apple will *try* to filter out adult content. If this is a young child, then a better option might be picking the web pages they can access—you could, for instance, block every Internet website except Disney. The next tab is People. This lets you select who they can email and message—you could limit them to only emailing parents and grandparents, for instance. The second to last tab lets you pick time limits. You can pick when they use the computer and for how long. And finally the last tab lets you turn off the camera so they can do video chatting, hide profanity from the dictionary, etc.

Accessibility

Accessibility helps you adjust the computer if you have any kind of impairment or disability. It lets you change things like making the display larger, having a voiceover that describes what's on your screen, and put captions on videos when available.

To open Accessibility, click System Settings and Accessibility. On the left side of the box that comes up will be all the various things you can change. Clicking on each one will create more options.

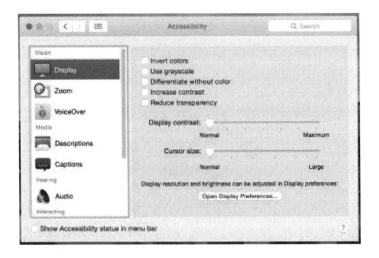

Vision
Under Display, you can make the screen grayscale, invert colors, decrease the contrast, etc.
Zoom allows you to create a zoom effect over smaller areas of the screen when you hit a
keyboard shortcut. VoiceOver reads back any text that's on the screen.

Media
The Media section includes a few different settings for audio and video playback. Click on
Descriptions to enable spoken descriptions for videos.

Captions will apply subtitles and captions to videos.

Hearing
The Sound tab provides options for the hearing disabled. You can choose to set up a visual
flash of the screen each time an alert sound is played, and also decide if you'd like to play
stereo audio as mono instead.

Interacting
Keyboard includes settings for Sticky Keys and Slow Keys. Sticky Keys allows certain
buttons to remain activated without you having to hold down the key. For example, if you
have Sticky Keys turned on and want to copy some text, instead of holding down Command +
C at the same time, you could press the Command button first, followed by the C key. When
enabled, you'll hear a lock sound, and anytime you use a modifier key like Command, a large
icon will appear in the top right corner of the screen indicating that a Sticky Key combination
has been started. Slow Keys increases the amount of time between a button press and
activation, so if you press Enter, it will take a little longer to actually process.

Mouse & Trackpad features settings like Mouse Keys, which lets you move the mouse around
using the number pad on your keyboard, double-click speed, and the option to ignore the
built-in trackpad (on MacBooks) if there is a separate mouse or trackpad connected to the
computer.

Switch Control requires you to enter your administrator before making any changes, because
it's a powerful function that allows you to control the computer using one or more switches
that you designate. You can also modify other settings like what to do while navigating,
determine pointer precision, and change the size for the Switch Control cursor.

The Dictation tab does exactly what it sounds like – it lets you dictate commands and write or edit text using only your voice. To enable dictation, you first need to click on the bottom button that says Open Dictation & Speech Preferences and selecting the On radio button.

Privacy and Security

If your computer is in a place where other people can get to it, or if you are just generally concerned about your privacy being violated, then head on over to Privacy and Security in the System Preferences.

Creating Strong Passwords

Strong passwords are the first line of defense against potential hackers (or smart children!); a strong password is not something like "password"; a strong password has letters, numbers and even symbols in it. It could be something like this: "@mY_MACb00k."

You can use the Password Assistant to test how strong your password is.

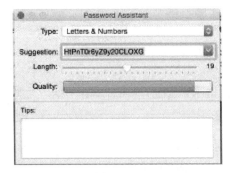

1. When Keychain loads, you will be able to view the entire list of accounts that are already synced to Keychain. If you would like to change the password for an account that already exists, find the account and double click on it. If not, click on the + button at the bottom to add a new account.

2. When the new window comes up, take a look at the bottom. There will be a field for password, and at the right of it will be a small key icon. Click the key icon to open up Password Assistant.

3. From Type you can select Manual (create your own), Memorable, Letters & Numbers, Numbers Only, Random, and FIPS-181 compliant.

4. Suggestions will automatically populate, and you can scroll through several different suggestions by using the dropdown menu.

5. Adjust the length slider to make the password longer or shorter. Any password you create will meet at least the requirements to be considered fair.

6. As you generate a password, the quality indicator will change to show you how safe and complex a given password is.

Firewall

Another line of defense you can add is a Firewall, which protects you from unwanted connections to potentially malicious software applications, websites, or files.

To enable the firewall that comes with your Mac, go to System Preferences > Security & Privacy and select the Firewall tab. Before you can make any changes, click on the lock icon in the bottom left corner and enter your administrator password to continue.

Find My Mac

Just like your iPhone or iPad, Mac comes with a handy feature called "Find My Mac" which lets you find your computer if someone steals it or you just misplace it; you can also wipe its hard drive clean remotely.

To enable Find My Mac, go to System Preferences > iCloud and check the box next to Find My Mac. Your location services must also be turned on, so go to System Preferences > Security & Privacy > Privacy > Location Services and make sure Enable Location Services is checked on.

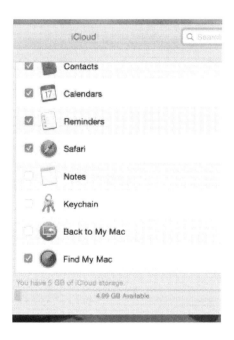

To track your computer, you can log into any computer and visit icloud.com, enter your iCloud login information, and click on Find My Mac. As long as the Mac is awake and connected to the Internet through Wi-Fi or Ethernet, you will be able to play loud sound, lock it, or completely erase it so your private information is removed.

Privacy

Apple knows people worry about privacy; they have lots built in to help you control what can (and can't) be seen.

Internet Privacy

If you'd like to clear your search and browsing history, there are two ways to do it: either by clicking on Safari > Clear History and Website Data or History > Clear History and Website Data. Both can be found on the top menu bar. When the window comes up, you will be able to choose how far back you want the clearing to reach, and once you make a selection, just press the Clear History button to make the changes final.

Cookies allow websites to store data and track certain things, like what other websites you visit during your Internet session, or what kind of products you tend to look at the most. This information is mostly used by advertisers to better target ads for you, but the option is always there if you'd like to disable them. Open up Safari, go to Safari > Preferences, then select the Privacy tab. The cookie options range from allowing all websites to store cookies to blocking all websites. You can also allow cookies only from the most frequently visited websites. If you prefer not to be tracked, check off the box at the bottom that says Ask Websites To Not Track Me. Some websites will not function as you may want them by disabling this feature.

Application Privacy
The other part of privacy is through installed applications. Go to System Preferences > Security & Privacy and click the Privacy tab. You can shut Location Services off by checking the box next to Enable Location Services. Browse through the left sidebar and you'll be able to customize permissions. If you don't want any apps to access your contacts or calendars, here is where you can block some or all programs from that information.

Part 3: Maintenance

Preserving Battery Life

If you are using an iMac, then this section will obviously not apply since iMacs don't run on battery, but if you have a MacBook, then this section for you.

Most MacBooks can easily get over 6 hours of battery life, but there are things you can do to get even more.

- Go to System Preferences > Energy Saver and under the Battery tab, choose to put hard disks to sleep whenever possible, and dim the display slightly while on battery power. You don't want to set it too low, or you'll find it going to sleep when you are reading or doing a task that doesn't require movement.

- Keep the screen only as bright as you need to clearly see the screen. The F1 key will minimalize the brightness and F2 will make it bright again. If you are at the beach then you will want the brightest, of course; but if you are in a dark room do you really need full brightness? Probably not.

- The keyboard also has brightness that can be adjusted with F5 and F6 on your keyboard. Backlight on the keyboard really helps in a lowlight setting, but when it's broad daylight, you really don't need it—even at the brightest, you probably would not even be able to tell that it's on.

- When you run websites with Flash, you are killing your battery. Be cautious of what you are using—especially if you are low on battery.

iCloud

iCloud lets you store things like photos and videos online. It's kind of like Google Drive or Dropbox. Best of all you get 5GB for free. Lots of cloud-based storage sites give you more storage than Apple—so why use it?

- You'll be able to back up your contacts so they are synced perfectly across your Mac, iPhone, iPad, and iPod. Make a change in a contact card or add a new contact, and the change or addition will be reflected across all of your synced iCloud devices.

- Media files purchased through the iTunes Store won't count against your storage.

- It makes files available across all of your Mac devices.

If you haven't set up an iCloud account, you can create one by going to System Preferences > iCloud and following the on screen instructions. Once you're finished, you'll be able to select what kind of data you'd like synced through iCloud: Photos, Mail, Contacts, Calendars, Safari, Notes, Keychain, and more. At the bottom you will notice a bar that indicates how much storage has been used up, and how much available storage you have left.

If you want more storage, you can pay extra. The following are the rates as of this writing:

- 20 GB for $0.99 a month
- 200 GB for $3.99 a month
- 500 GB for $9.99 a month
- 1 TB for $19.99 a month

If you decide to change your mind and don't need the extra storage plans, Apple gives you 15 days to contact them and ask for a refund.

Time Machine

Everyone worries about losing their data; Apple helps you out with one of their most powerful behind-the-scenes apps: Time Machine.

Time Machine will back up all of your files, applications, and settings with minimal configuration or headache. In the case of a catastrophic event such as hard drive failure, having a Time Machine backup can allow you to quickly recover all of your data and applications, and even all of your settings (such as your desktop background and even the specific location of icons on your desktop).

You will need to buy an external USB or Thunderbolt hard drive. It is recommended to buy a drive that is larger than the current used space on your computer. For example, if you have used 100 gigabytes of space on your computer's hard drive, you should buy at least a 120 gigabyte hard drive.

You can also purchase an additional Time Machine Airport Capsule that does all of this wirelessly.

To get started, plug the hard drive into your computer and Time Machine will start automatically. It will ask you if you would like to use the drive as a Time Machine Backup Disk. Choose "Use as Backup Disk".

If Time Machine does not start automatically, go to Finder > Applications > Machine, and click "Choose Backup Disk". Select your new hard drive.

After you specify the drive to use as a backup, Time Machine will automatically begin backing up your data.

Software Updates

If you want your computer running smoothly then make sure you update regularly; updates are free and come once every couple of months. They fix minor bugs and sometimes add things to correct vulnerabilities that might make your computer open to viruses.

Mac OS X, by default, will prompt you when updates are available, and you need only to click "Update" and enter your password in order to run the updates. Sometimes, in the case of major updates, you will need to restart your computer to complete the update. You can click "Not now" if you would like to delay the updates until a more convenient time.

Appendix A: Keyboard Shortcuts

General Shortcuts

Command-X – Cuts or removes selected text or item and copies it to the clipboard.
Command-C – Copies the selected text or item to the clipboard.
Command-V – Pastes the contents of the clipboard into the document, app, or finder.
Command-Z – Undoes the previous command.
Command- Shift-Z – Redoes the previous undo.
Command-A – Selects all text or items in the running program.
Command-F – Opens the Find window to find documents or other items.
Command-G – Finds the next occurrence of a previously found item (i.e. Find Again).
Command-H – Hides the current running program or front window (Note: this will not work if you have a program running in full screen).
Command-Option-H – Hides all the open apps and windows.
Command-M – Minimizes the currently open window or app (Note: this will not work if you have a program running in full screen).
Command-Option-M – Minimizes all open apps and windows.
Command-N – Opens a new document or window.
Command-O – Opens an item (for instance if you are in Word or Pages and you want to open a previously saved document).
Command-P – Print the current website or document.
Command-S – Save the current document.
Command-W – Close the front window or app
Command-Option-W – Close all open apps and windows.
Command-Q – Quit an app.
Command-Option-Esc – Force quit a program that is not responding.
Command-Space Bar – Brings up Spotlight to quickly find documents, emails, and apps.
Command-Tab – Switch to the next open app (Note: if you don't let go of Command and continue hitting the Tab button, you can continue going to the next app.
Command-Shift-3 – Take a screenshot of your entire screen.
Command-, – Opens the Preference menu (if applicable) for the current app.

Document Shortcuts

The following shortcuts are applicable to supported document software like Word, PowerPoint, Pages, Excel, OpenOffice, etc.

Command-B – Bold or un-bold the selected text.
Command-I – Italicize or un-italics selected text.
Command-U – Underline or remove underline to selected text.

50135418R00051

Made in the USA
San Bernardino, CA
14 June 2017